Mr. &

ALSO BY JAMESON FITZPATRICK

Morrisroe: Erasures

Mr. &

POEMS

Jameson Fitzpatrick

INDOLENT BOOKS

© 2018 Jameson Fitzpatrick

Author photo: Jacques Servin

Cover and book design: adam b. bohannon

Book editor: Michael Broder

Published by Indolent Books,

an imprint of Indolent Arts Foundation, Inc.

www.indolentbooks.com

Brooklyn, New York

ISBN-13: 978-1-945023-17-0

for the wives

CONTENTS

The Genius of Wives I Have Sat With

Before I decided to write this, I had often said that I would. I had often said that I would write, then not sat down to do it. I had often sat that I would write and still not written what I had said I would, The genius of wives of geniuses I have sat with. I have sat so much with so many. I have sat with wives who were neither wives nor geniuses, of geniuses who were wives. I have sat with real wives who were geniuses, of geniuses who were not real, wives, geniuses, or otherwise. I have sat with wives who were not wives but were geniuses, of geniuses who may or may not have been wives, geniuses, or real. I have sat with wives of geniuses, near wives of geniuses, with wives of near geniuses, of would be geniuses, of literary and evil and mad geniuses. I have been a wife who was not a real wife, of a genius who was a real asshole. I mean genius. He was how I came to sit with the many real geniuses and the many wives who were not real wives but were more often than not the real geniuses. In short, I have sat very often and very long with myself.

(Pre)Nuptials

(1) hereinafter & hereby
Prospective Band & Prospective If
con the nearest wish

(2) regarding income & property
separately or together
the Prospectors have made

(3) liabilities of each other
whereas each of the parties must provide
whereas each of the parties desires

(4) to own & hold, acquire & dispose of
as though unmarried, respective
in accordance with his or her own future

(5) unhappy differences may arise

3

       division of rope

       whether currently held or hereafter

(6) If would like Band's yellow shirt

       torn in two places

       with the collar stitched up &

(7) Band would also like it,

       If in his yellow shirt

       torn in two

(8) places to be allocated as follows:

       his his his his his

       If can have Brooklyn

(9) Band can have his baby & his many men

       If can have none of them

       both halves the double bed

(10) in the event of irreconcilable perspectives

       the parties did execute voluntarily

       the parties did end

Mr. &

Reader, I married him.

the ladle with which she was basting
suspended in air
the same space of time
knives also had rest
fully explaining also why I had thus acted.
I am my husband's As Fully
his As Free As In Solitude
his As Gay As In Company
then his vision, as I am still
putting into words the effect
of the landscape of his ear
where he wished to go
what he wished to be done
There was a pleasure in my service
that to yield was to be ambitious yet

I felt, I remember

little perk of self-approbation with which

fulfillment means disaster

a cold hand came on

startled to begin with

close together in front of the steps up to

    the house

You're Mrs. [Page 148]

Meantime—this man

otherwise delirium

to quit when I was happy and beloved

was dear to me

wandering limbs

trace the steps of my grief

him I must drag

on the grass and kiss

that my vow was heard and that I was reserved

would not consent, formally

He had an aversion
to choosing sustenance
'Night-walking amuses him, then'
He took his knife and fork
a strong thrilling
Mr. leaning against the ledge
in his familiar voice
incarnate infancy
the little dark thing
I found it locked

at intervals, an anxious feeling

momentary doubt of its being possible to
    be cured of her attachment
and really, it was not long
every day was giving her fresh reason
a very promising step of the mind on its way
    to resignation
Within a month
very little white satin
But, in spite of these deficiencies

felicity in so unusual a form

Mr. missed exceedingly his affection

Mr. Half As Well As I Do My Dear

Mr. so near a vicinity

to her very material advantage

the promise of balls and young men

suspected by her father

she could still moralize every morning

their characters suffered

He bore

It is a great comfort to have you so rich

Her father had been looking at her

Who is that

in her pink almost

people getting emptier and emptier

scattered rather

That did make her happy.

brain matter

heart come

but for a moment this terror

this ecstasy he thought to himself

her Professor

loved occasionally

out of respect to his former mistress

a wilderness of boys

little ragamuffins

the most beautiful things

being the sauce best beloved by the boyish

    soul

these unromantic facts

They began

down the old pace
into moments when
she seemed to be sitting beside her lover
transitory sensation of slipping
Mr. seldom spoke
Mr. denuded
pencilled in as December
to whom something irreparable had happened
at Mr.'s side the strain of
no room in her mind
He filled her cup and plate
stray address
his hands behind his head
a lady who was probably his wife
opened a book in a bedroom
on the fifth floor
He had gone to the barber's
why should she not tell him the truth?

man-high

large black car would drive me
at the wrought-iron heart
of the old landscape left off
Everybody would know about me
gingerly
with my mother's face
martyr's smile
Maybe forgetfulness
"A man to see you!"
"A man to see you!"
on the glassy rim
that expanse
of grateful snowdrift
cup in the saucer with an awkward clatter
his face like a tonic
or a six-foot-deep gap

84

today
I saw no point
to him
on the whole
I concentrate
the way light would
on a windowsill
I threw the coins in
the water in such a way
I almost moved.
I refrained.
in my defense
I know "nothing"

A few weeks late

Mr. knocked on my door, told me

he had been feeling uneasy

we'd held the Ugly Pain Competition

We discussed it: Was the winner of an Ugly
    Pain

the person who made the uglier pain

or the person who made pain
    inadvertently?

Did I want to come with them?

up to the observation deck we arranged
    ourselves

like stroke marks left behind by the players

dark roots from above

drinking from our bottles very heavily.

They bent low, one threw himself to the
    ground

and missed. We turned our attention

to anything but explosions, his sweet tic

that night

long tears fell
on the children's chairs
a flood
of mathematics
and choice
after her brother made his decision
they both pledged themselves
more than children
the blank suburban space
they were supposed to

since it was the fashion to be in love
with married people

she could run away any time
she intended to hammer his head into a jelly
a little travel-stained
over those loose planks last summer
packing away his tools
a little swim, before dinner
There was no one thing in the world she
    desired.
Like antagonists that had overcome her
she knew a way to elude them
her old bathing suit still hanging
the night she swam out
the blue-grass meadow

hunting, rifles, mechanics, cars

he'd get furious about
getting eaten by tigers
or getting drowned in the river
the supernatural light that follows
This bend or branch
too expensive for my mother
but with him scarcely
Chance did not forget
"the happiest days of her life"
more tragic than they are today.
He behaved as usual
water from the jars
called me his child.

fifty still dreams

but not of his feet on the desk
the dimmer dusty older he gets
occasional imperative
to amble bearish into infinitude
a lapse he thinks of as "his book"
her version of his life
an oddly repellant love poem.
He has resisted the middle-aged
tendency to retreat,
the model's secret pride.
Sometimes he shuts the book he is
such an unprepossessing object.
I can move him no further from me.

The Definition of

marriage is not beautiful

marriage is hard

marriage is a private affair

marriage is over

marriage is a crazy thing

marriage is not a 24-hour repair shop

marriage is to be at peace with someone
within four walls

marriage is beautiful

marriage is a little bit like that nice cup of
coffee

marriage is recommended or compulsory

marriage is damaged by bomb

marriage is the process by which

marriage is profoundly connected to health

marriage is really weird

marriage is and why it matters

marriage is not marriage

marriage is a fraud

marriage is legal

marriage is the law of the land

marriage is not beyond those rights

marriage is confined

marriage is a perversion of the institution

marriage is slowly expanding

marriage is here

marriage is protected

marriage is not among those rights

marriage is wrong

marriage is only the beginning

marriage is an expression of

marriage is outlawed

marriage is certainly very wrong

marriage is not endorsed

marriage is a slippery slope

marriage is more political than pastoral

marriage is polygamy

marriage is finally

marriage is proper and indeed essential

marriage is not sexual

marriage is based on perceptions

marriage is not really about

marriage is not enough

marriage is not sanctioned

marriage is blasphemy

marriage is a demonic ceremony

marriage is a Marxist plot

marriage is ordered

marriage is inevitable

marriage is a good idea

marriage is in contradiction

marriage is a recent phenomenon

marriage is recognized

marriage is already

marriage is really ultimately

marriage is their only real path

marriage is useful

marriage is functionally

marriage is good for children

marriage is a human rights violation

marriage is a traditional practice

marriage is embedded in the customs

marriage is much less of an issue in the US

marriage is poverty

marriage is widespread

marriage is a death sentence

marriage is an issue which affects girls in
    every country

marriage is not an intractable tradition

marriage is irrevocably entrenched

marriage is often regarded as necessary

marriage is rape culture

marriage is harmful

marriage is a curse

marriage is deeply rooted

marriage is a major psychological trauma

marriage is common

marriage is a violence

marriage is getting renewed

marriage is a term employed

marriage is a phrase that refers to

marriage is shown by the fact that

marriage is killing traditional marriage

marriage is total bullshit

marriage is usually so fecund

marriage is not just about marriage

marriage is arguing for a return

marriage is just one option

marriage is religious dogma

marriage is to be sad and dutiful

marriage is losing

marriage is now in jeopardy

marriage is fuller social calendars

marriage is like a tree planted

marriage is like building a house

marriage is like a deck of cards

marriage is like a garden

marriage is like a horse race

marriage is like a circle

marriage is like a workshop

marriage is like the IKEA of relationships

marriage is like watching the color of the
    leaves

marriage is like a marshmallow

marriage is like music

marriage is like a dance

marriage is like training for the Olympics

marriage is like business

marriage is like legalizing pot

marriage is like fine wine

marriage is like a cage

marriage is like a pickle

marriage is like the devil taking control

marriage is like that

marriage is the union of two forgivers

marriage is a lifetime of hands

marriage is a novella by Stephen King

marriage is made by keeping

marriage is one which allows for

marriage is the enemy of a great marriage

marriage is to maintain the magic ratio

marriage is not 50-50

marriage is rated R

marriage is broken

marriage is a mess

marriage is in shambles

marriage is killing me

marriage is my idol

marriage is my biggest accomplishment

marriage is my letting God be my God

marriage is my love lock

marriage is my mirror

marriage is my literary material

marriage is my marriage

marriage is my business

marriage is my desert

marriage is my cross

Vow

your strange unto me   to Write or
to   Excuse   my   ancient   Message
by   your   Command   your   poor   wife
proceeded   to   Name   and   Place
willingly   as if   Pleasure had been
so pleased   you   have   chosen me
from low desire   bad stain   but let
me   have   no   open   shame   but to
follow   your   Affection   already
settled on my Suspicion   you have
your   Happiness   the   Instruments
thereof   your unprincely   and   cruel
usage of me   whatsoever the world
may think   my last   and only   self
may not touch those poor Gentle-
men   for my sake   if ever I found
the   Name   pleasing   then   let   me

trouble   your   Grace   in   all   your
Actions   your   most   Loyal   and   ever
Prison   Tower

W/O

to have and withhold
from this day forward
to withstand before you today
do you take
do you take

without ceremony, without witness
without license or signet or judge

without captain or charter
garter or stocks
without falter or father or farce

without this ring
I thee whet
unlawfully
without trophy

to speke of wo that is
without marriage
speak now
or forever withhold your peace
unpronounce us man &

stealing off the bridle path
(newly weeded, newly wet)
to wait for better or worse

without lace or slip or train
trip or isle
without flute or sip or song
without moon without honey

save the datesweet
nothing to savor
further up the later trail
no reception no
receiving line

without death

without dew

without us

without part

remove this title

from the man I love

like a veil if you can lift it

NOTES & ACKNOWLEDGMENTS

Thank you to the editors of *Pinwheel* and *Poor Claudia*, where sections of "Mr. &" first appeared, and to Harry Burke for including "The Definition of" in a poetry mixtape for the exhibition "Works Off Paper" at SALTS, Birsfelden (as "Definitions").

"The Genius of Wives of Geniuses I Have Sat With" is after a paragraph in Gertrude Stein's *The Autobiography of Alice B. Toklas*.

The fragments of "Mr. &" draw their language, respectively, from the final chapters of the following books: *Jane Eyre* by Charlotte Brontë, *The Return of the Soldier* by Rebecca West, *Frankenstein; or, The Modern Prometheus* by Mary Shelley, *Wuthering Heights* by Emily Brontë, *Emma* by Jane Austen, *Pride and Prejudice* by Jane Austen, *Mrs. Dalloway* by Virginia Woolf, *Little Women* by Louisa May Alcott, *Summer* by Edith Wharton, *The Bell Jar* by Sylvia Plath, *Play It As It Lays* by Joan Didion, *How Should A Person Be?* by Sheila Heti, *Summer Rain* by Marguerite Duras, *The Awakening* by Kate Chopin, *The Lover* by Marguerite Duras, and *Asa, As I Knew Him* by Susanna Kaysen.

"The Definition of" comprises various Google results for different manipulations of the phrase "marriage is."

"Vow" draws its language from what is thought to be Anne Boleyn's last letter to her husband Henry VIII, written while she was awaiting execution at the Tower of London.

ABOUT THE AUTHOR

Jameson Fitzpatrick is the author of the chapbook *Morrisroe: Erasures* (89plus/LUMA Publications, 2014). His poems have appeared in *Best New Poets 2017*, *The New Yorker*, *Poetry*, and elsewhere. A 2017 NYSCA/NYFA Fellow in Poetry, he lives in New York City and teaches writing at New York University.

ABOUT INDOLENT BOOKS

Indolent Books is a small nonprofit poetry press based in Brooklyn. Indolent publishes poetry by underrepresented voices whose work is innovative, provocative, and risky, and that uses all the resources of poetry to address urgent racial, social, and economic justice concerns.

Lightning Source UK Ltd.
Milton Keynes UK
UKHW04f0316170818
327306UK00042B/1305P